THE
NORTH-SOUTH DIVIDE

A coast to coast from Aberystwyth
to Southwold

by Mountain Bike

Vince Major

Published by Vince Major

Publishing partner: Paragon Publishing, Rothersthorpe

ISBN 978-1-78792-042-2

Book design, layout and production management by Into Print
www.intoprint.net
01604 832149

Cover photo
Location: Burrough Hill, Leicestershire

Disclaimer
Every effort has been made to achieve accuracy of information for use in this guidebook. The author and publisher can take no responsibility or liability for any loss (including fatal), damage or trespass as a result of the route information or advice offered in this guidebook.

The inclusion of a path or track in this guide does not guarantee it remains a right of way. If conflict with a land owner occurs, please leave by the shortest possible route available and inform the relevant authority if deemed necessary.

Please follow the country code and always give way to pedestrians and horses.

CONTENTS

WHAT'S IN THIS BOOK?

Route descriptions, maps, charts and statistics form the basis of this book.

Other useful information about bikes, kit, logistics, accommodation, local bike shops, cafes and other refreshment stops are also included.

Much of the accommodation and cafes have been tried and tested by us personally, whether on recce missions or on the events we've previously organised on this route.

'NSD – the beginning' is a chapter about how this route came about, detailing the methods used to piece it together.

Other information on 'Places of Interest' has also been included. These are an eclectic mix that range from brewery tours to bridges!

Another chapter is about some of the riders (in their own words) who rode the route on our May 2023 event.

THE NORTH-SOUTH DIVIDE OVERVIEW

The NSD is an unusual but interesting route spanning west to east across the central belt of the UK that takes in a contrast of landscapes from the **Cambrian Mountains** in **Wales** to the **Fens** in **East Anglia** and everything in between.

Starting at the well-known university town of **Aberystwyth** on the west Wales coast, then finishing at the quintessentially British, old-fashioned seaside town of **Southwold** on the Suffolk coast.

Some of the many highlights include the wild and remote Welsh mountains, the equally sparse **Kerry Ridgeway**, the Shropshire Hills including the **Long Mynd** and **Wenlock Edge**, the **Ironbridge Gorge**, **Cannock Chase**, the **National Forest** and the UK's largest lowland pine forest at **Thetford** in the heart of East Anglia.

This **360 mile (579km)** route with over **20,000 feet (7,000m)** of elevation gain will take you through **Ceredigion, Powys, Shropshire, Staffordshire, Derbyshire, Leicestershire, Rutland, Northamptonshire, Cambridgeshire, Norfolk** and **Suffolk.**

MAP OVERVIEW

ELEVATION

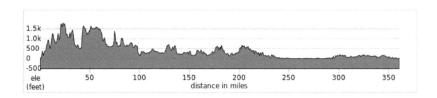

SUPPORTED OR UNSUPPORTED

Supported or unsupported? That is the question...

For many reasons, a supported ride is the easier and less stressful option to ride the NSD. A support vehicle can carry all your luggage and many other items including bike spare parts, a bike stand, spare wheels, tyres, tools, bike cleaning equipment, camping gear etc., even a spare bike! All of this means you only need to carry what is necessary for a day ride. The support can be there when you need it for major mechanicals, other emergencies and to transport all your gear to the next overnight stop. For these reasons you can confidently book accommodation well in advance knowing you will arrive at your destination and not lose deposits or having to find last minute places to stay – not much fun after you've been riding for 8 hours or longer!

An unsupported option would perhaps give you a greater sense of adventure. With the current craze of bikepacking, there's a lot of lightweight equipment on the market for rides of this nature, however an estimate of the load you would carry on the bike would be three to four times heavier on an unsupported trip. There are some things you can do to help on an unsupported trip, for example, mailing fresh clothing ahead to places that you know you'll stay at, along with stamped addressed packages to mail gear home. A mountain bike trailer would not be suitable on the NSD.

NORTH-SOUTH DIVIDE
- THE BEGINNING

The idea of creating this route began by discovering how good some of the central areas of England are as a mountain biking destination. Living in the East Midlands means that my riding mates and I often go to places like the Long Mynd, Cannock Chase and the National Forest area in South Derbyshire and Leicestershire. When you add the Welsh mountains, Wenlock Edge, the Ironbridge Gorge and the historical areas of Rockingham Forest and Rutland, there is a base to work from!

And then, adding the three trail centres at Nant yr Arian, Cannock Chase and Thetford Forest, the route really started to take shape.

So, with the existing knowledge of several well-ridden areas, my usual route-finding process got under way. Looking at Ordnance Survey maps, researching magazines and the internet to find the best places to ride, plus utilising Strava segment explorer, Strava heat maps and Google Earth, all of which are excellent route creating tools. These can all help to create the basis of a route, but you've still got to get out there – the best bit of course!

It was great fun exploring this 'central belt' of England and Wales. I especially enjoyed discovering the lesser-known off-road delights of Mid-Wales around Llanidloes and East Shropshire including Caer Caradoc, situated next to the A49 opposite the much-more-ridden Long Mynd.

Staffordshire, west of Cannock Chase, was another new area along with the East Anglian Fens and the depths of a previously unknown Suffolk.

I find it particularly interesting to ride and explore an

area that a lot of us have driven through many times to get to the more well-known and popular riding spots.

It possibly took around twenty trips to finalise the route, racking up several thousand miles of travelling by road and rail plus over 800 miles of riding!

The name of the route is a well-known phrase and an obvious choice really, and suits it perfectly...

KIT

The kit lists that follow will provide you with a rough idea of what you will need on a trip like this.

Bike

The ideal bike for this trip would be a lightweight, short-travel, full suspension mountain bike. An equivalent hardtail would also be fine but not quite as comfortable. A gravel bike would also be suitable but not as much fun as a MTB, plus you would need to be prepared for some of the gnarly and rough sections!

A bike with more than 130mm travel is probably not that suitable.

Tubeless tyres or 'sealant' type tubes are a good idea to prevent punctures. Disc brakes are also a good option. Whichever bike you choose, it needs to be in excellent working order because this route is hard on machinery especially if wet and muddy.

Bike Spares

If you are attempting this ride unsupported, then you are limited to what you can carry, though riding in a group means you can share the load.

If you have a support vehicle, then bike spares are not an issue, just take everything!

Essentials for an unsupported trip could be:
- Tyre levers
- Spare tubes
- Tyre boot (for split tyre repair)

- Pump
- Patches/tubeless repair kit
- Multi-tool (inc. chain splitter and spoke key)
- Spare brake pads
- Gaffer tape (wound around pump)
- Cable ties (various lengths)
- Mech hanger (specific to your bike)
- Gear cable
- Chain links/pins
- Spare spokes x 3 (correct length)
- Small narrow cleaning brush
- Small bottle of lube
- Rag
- Lightweight bike lock
- Small rear light
- Small but punchy front light

Clothing

If you are planning on carrying all your gear, on bike and après bike, then technical, lightweight materials are best.

Navigation

A GPS unit with the relevant mapping is a huge asset when tackling a big ride like the NSD. It's not essential to have a GPS, but with the route uploaded onto the unit, it will save a lot of time out on the trail.

GPX files can be found at **www.mtbepicsuk.co.uk/gps** However, you will still need traditional maps as they can often prove invaluable when you need the 'bigger picture' or to find an alternative route. **Ordnance Survey Landranger 1:50,000** maps are recommended on this trip and generally have enough detail. The twelve maps required to cover this route are as follows (in order of the route)

Numbers are: 135-138, 127-129, 141-144 & 156.

All these maps would cost a fair bit of money to buy but there are alternatives, see below.

Please Note:

The OS maps showing this route (PDF files) can be found on our website to download or print off. It's recommended to download them onto your smartphone where you can zoom in to enlarge details and not lose clarity. These files can be found at **www.mtbepicsuk.co.uk/maps**

OS maps can also be borrowed from local libraries.

A compass and knowing how to use it is always worth having too.

First Aid Kit

As an experienced mountain biker you may know the basics of first aid, what should be in the kit and how to use it. It would be a good idea to read up and remind yourself of first aid procedures before the trip.

The most common problems encountered can be cuts, grazes, exposure, a broken or cracked collar bone, sunburn and saddle sores!

One addition to a first aid kit could be a tick removal tool (Pets Buddy sold on Amazon is ideal). Ticks can be a danger to your health if not dealt with correctly. DO NOT SQUEEZE A TICK WHEN ATTEMPTING TO REMOVE. Using a correct tool reduces the risk of an infection like Lyme Disease.

Miscellaneous

- A bladder type hydration system or bottles
- Bell or whistle
- Small sewing kit (for torn clothes or tyre)
- Lip balm
- Sunscreen (At least SPF 30)
- Ear plugs (for a good night's sleep!)
- Chargers for GPS and phone
- Weatherproof bags (for phone and clothes etc.)

Please note:
These lists are not definitive and simply provide a pointer.

TRAVEL AND ACCOMMODATION

Logistics

The NSD is designed to start in Aberystwyth and should be ridden in the correct West to East direction as there are many descents (and climbs) that have been strategically added to maximize the fun aspect to the route. The three trail centres en-route can only be ridden in a certain direction too.

Trains

There are many options of how to travel to and from the start and finish points of the NSD by train. Here are a few pointers:

- Aberystwyth has a good regular train service especially from Birmingham.
- The nearest train station to Southwold is Halesworth which is approx. 5 miles away and can be reached from Liverpool St. station in London.
- Halesworth can also connect with the Midlands via Norwich using the 'Crosscountry' rail link service.

There are many other stations either on or close by along the route too in case of an emergency or a need to bail. These are all listed in the directory found further on in this guide.

- www.nationalrail.co.uk
  The official source for UK train times and other information.
- www.thetrainline.com
  Excellent phone app for times and fares.

- www.atob.org.uk
  Information on train companies and their policies on bike carriage.

Please note:
More than two people with bikes on trains could encounter problems. One way to avoid this and/or having to book and reserve a (potentially limited) place for your bike, is to use foldable bike bags and mail them from Aberystwyth to the accommodation you choose at the Southwold end.

A homemade bike bag is easy to make using strong plastic sheeting, bubble wrap, gaffer tape and some rope or similar for a shoulder strap.

Duration

The NSD would work well as a 6-7 day ride for most people, with the average 50 miles (80.5km) and 3,000 – 5,000 feet (900 – 1,500m) of elevation gain each day providing a decent challenge. However, the super-fit could ride it in perhaps two or three days – though not too many could ride this in one hit! Others may choose to spend two weeks over it and really take in the fantastic scenery and history.

Accommodation

Unsupported rides of this length are difficult to plan ahead because of so many unforeseen circumstances. The only certainty is the start point. It is recommended that any accommodation, however you plan to ride this route, is booked at least 3 months in advance to avoid disappointment.

We have some recommendations listed in a directory.

These are mainly based on places we've personally stayed at and/or used on the events we've previously organised.

NORTH-SOUTH DIVIDE
BY NUMBERS

- **362 total miles (583km)**

- **152 off-road miles (230km)**

- **21,092ft total elevation gain (6,428m)**

- **1,768ft highest point (539m)**

- **156 off-road sections**

- **3 trail centres**

- **11 counties**

- **13 towns**

- **2 countries**

- **2 piers**

- **1 world heritage site**

Burrough Hill, Leicestershire

Panoramic views across Shropshire

Vanishing point on the Fens

ROUTE DESCRIPTIONS

The overall route is split into seven sections.

1 - Aberystwyth to Llanidloes

2 - Llanidloes to Church Stretton

3 - Church Stretton to Cannock Chase

4 - Cannock Chase to Woodhouse Eaves

5 - Woodhouse Eaves to Farcet

6 - Farcet to Thetford

7 - Thetford to Southwold

Aberystwyth to Llanidloes

36.7 total miles (59.06km)
18.15 off-road miles (29.21km)
5,482ft elevation gain (1,671m)

Straight into the deep end with a crossing of the wild and remote Cambrian Mountains via the top-quality trail centre at Nant yr Arian.

The climbing begins as soon as you leave the promenade in Aberystwyth and it's up almost all the way on a variety of quiet roads and tracks to join the purpose-built MTB trails at Nant yr Arian. A big highlight here is the well-established and flowing 'Mark of Zorro' singletrack descent.

A quick road blast leads to another big climb up to an area of high, craggy upland forestry then up again to the Cefn Croes windfarm and the highest point of the North-South Divide at 1,768ft (539m). On a clear day, great views of the Irish Sea can be had from here.

A super-fast, eyeballs-out descent on forestry tracks follows, then onto a couple of sharp road climbs and off-road sections of doubletrack that will lead you to the traditional Welsh market town of Llanidloes – the first town on the famous River Severn.

Aberystwyth to Llanidloes

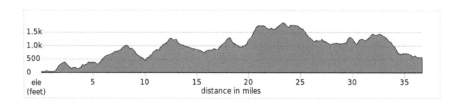

Llanidloes to Church Stretton

47.2 total miles (75.96km)
22.41 off-road miles (30.06)
4,385ft elevation gain (1,303m)

A bit of rough bridleway and a little section of forestry is first up upon leaving Llanidloes, before a huge climb, the biggest of the entire route, leads up to the massive Llandinam windfarm with its 103 turbines.

This leads to more tracks on the sparse Welsh Marches. Here, there are great views of the English/Welsh border from the Kerry Ridgeway, a high-level ancient drover's trail, that leads you into Shropshire with more remote bridleways and several good descents taking you to the small rural town of Bishops Castle.

Quiet lanes then take you towards the huge whaleback of the well-known Long Mynd that tops out at over 500 metres.

A long off-road climb takes you to Pole Bank which is the highest point of the Long Mynd at 516m, before a quick road section gets you to the top and the start point of the legendary Minton Batch. This sinuous ribbon of singletrack, often lauded in the MTB media as one of Britain's finest natural descents, leads to an easy cruise on quiet roads and into the busy and touristy Shropshire town of Church Stretton.

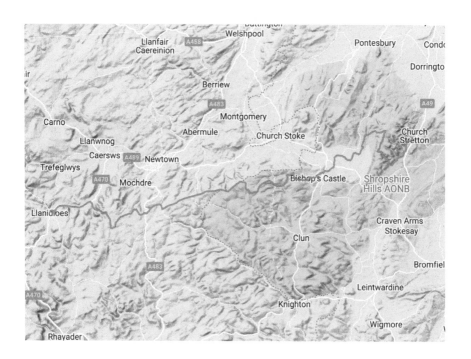

Llanidloes to Church Stretton

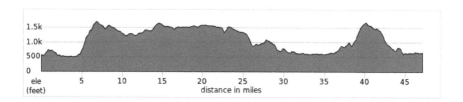

Church Stretton to Cannock Chase

47.6 total miles (76.6km)
20.37 off-road miles (32.94km)
2,696ft elevation gain (822m)

A good off-road start with some great views of the stunning Shropshire countryside near the ancient Caer Caradoc hill fort begin this section.

This is followed by a lengthy but easy cruise along the disused rail line on Wenlock Edge, culminating in a super-fast and fun descent into the small, historical town of Much Wenlock – credited for creating the modern Olympics.

A short road section then leads you to a long woodland descent to the river Severn at the world-famous Ironbridge Gorge – the birthplace of the industrial revolution. The stunning Ironbridge itself, the centrepiece of this World Heritage Site, is a great place to take a break.

Cross the Severn and into Staffordshire and on to quiet lanes and several off-road sections that lead to the busy, small town of Penkridge. An easy jaunt along the picturesque Staffordshire and Worcestershire canal and a short road section then takes you into the well-known and one of the best MTB destinations in the Midlands – Cannock Chase.

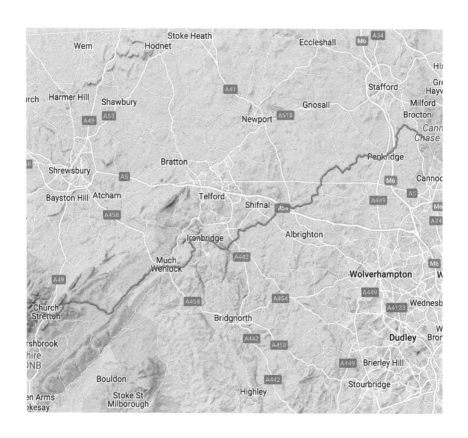

Church Stretton to Cannock Chase

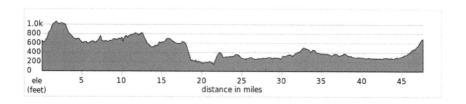

Cannock Chase to Woodhouse Eaves

56.3 total miles (90.6km)
28.76 off-road miles (46.20km)
3,527ft elevation gain (1,075m)

Ride across Cannock Chase on miles of different tracks including some fine purpose-built MTB trails that boast plenty of technical features. After leaving the forest, you'll skirt the town of Rugeley to join an interesting section of the Trent and Mersey canal and on to Burton upon Trent via quiet lanes and more off-road sections.

Once the beer brewing capital of the world, breweries are still prominent in Burton. Sadly, the popular National Brewery Museum has now closed but is due to relocate and re-open in the future. After passing the large Marstons brewery, ride through the town centre and cross the river Trent on the famous and unusual Ferry Bridge.

The surprisingly good trails then continue into South Derbyshire and the pleasant rolling countryside of the National Forest area which leads into rural and green Leicestershire on The Cloud Trail – a long disused rail line. Follow this into the Charnwood Forest area to join quiet lanes, cycle paths and bridleways that lead you to Beacon Hill Country Park with its craggy summit and fantastic views. A super-fast bridleway descent off Beacon Hill then leads to the village of Woodhouse Eaves which has a shop and several pubs.

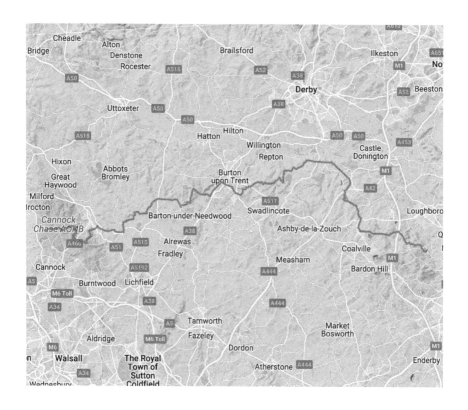

Cannock Chase to Woodhouse Eaves

Woodhouse Eaves to Farcet

55.8 total miles (89.8km)
19.26 off-road miles (31.01km)
2,517ft elevation gain (767m)

Next up is the scenic Swithland reservoir before joining a nice, flowy descent on disused mining tracks to Mountsorrel.

A road section follows through quintessential English towns and villages before things start to get lumpy again as you approach the old county of Rutland. A short climb up to the Iron Age hill fort on Burrough Hill follows with its good panoramic views, then quiet roads and some long off-road bridleways lead you towards the vast Rutland Water, the largest reservoir in England by surface area.

After passing close to the giant reservoir, a nice rural descent leads to the village of Wing, known for its stately Hall and a rare and ancient turf maze.

A very brief visit to my home county of Northants is next and begins with a quick blast on easy trails through Fineshade Woods which has excellent facilities. A string of picturesque villages in the historical Rockingham Forest area then leads you into Cambridgeshire where the scenery changes drastically.

Here you'll join the 'Green Wheel' – a long off-road cycle path that orbits Peterborough. A section of this will soon take you to the village of Farcet, situated on the edge of the Fens.

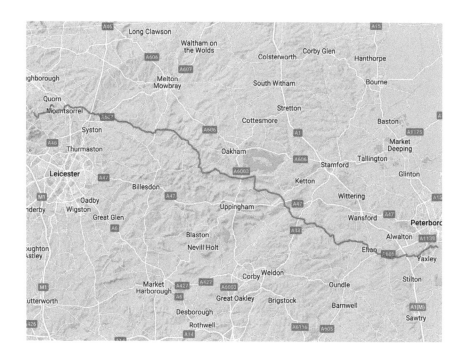

Woodhouse Eaves to Farcet

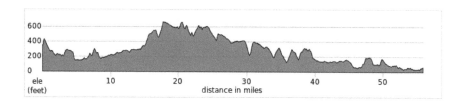

Farcet to Thetford

68 total miles (109.43km)
22.7 off-road miles (36.53km)
1,657ft elevation gain (505m)

The terrain now is pan flat with 'big sky' views along with some long off-road tracks, cycle paths and byway sections.

Continue into this Fenland landscape, often next to water and ride through the small Cambridgeshire towns of Whittlesey and March where both are a good place to stock up.

The Fens become more remote around the Welney and Southery areas and have many dead-straight roads and tracks known as droves. Eventually, the landscape changes as you enter The Brecks – a vast heathland area containing the huge expanse of Thetford Forest – the UK's largest lowland pine forest and East Anglia's premier MTB destination.

Sandy trails lead you into the Breckland town of Brandon before entering Thetford Forest. You'll wind through the forest on some very long stretches of undulating natural singletrack and purpose-built MTB trails that end on the edge of the historical town of Thetford. A short ride into town passes the priory remains before glimpsing the motte and bailey of the 900-year-old castle.

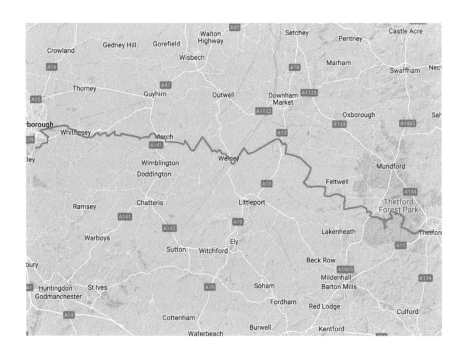

Farcet to Thetford

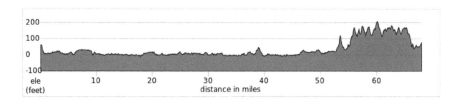

Thetford to Southwold

49.9 total miles (80.3km)
20.78 off-road miles (33.44km)
1,465ft elevation gain (447m)

After leaving the town of Thetford, a mix of quiet lanes and woodland tracks lead you out of Breckland and into the depths of Suffolk to join rural bridleways, byways and quiet roads through more quintessentially English countryside and on towards the East Anglian coast.

After passing through lots of villages and skirting the town of Halesworth, you'll pass the large expanse of the tidal river Blyth on some fine woodland and heathland singletrack bridleways. You'll then cross the river and ride through the interesting Southwold harbour area. This river harbour has many nautical sights as well as a couple of eateries and a pub.

The harbour kiosk, close to the sand dunes and beach, is a traditional seaside takeaway and is worth a stop as you might dip your wheel and/or self in the sea!

A short ride into Southwold to end this route finishes at St. James Green in the centre of town near the iconic lighthouse. The nearby Sole Bay Inn, opposite the well-known Adnams brewery, could be the place to toast the end of this epic...

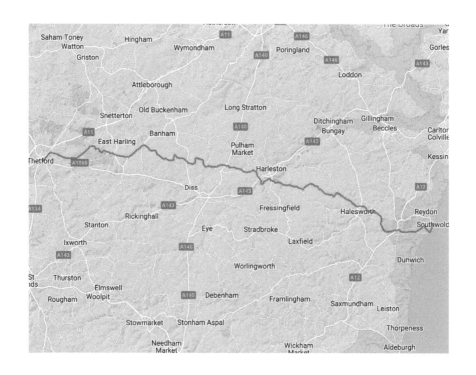

Thetford to Southwold

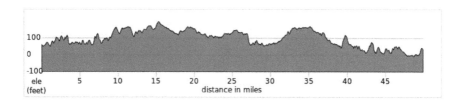

PLACES OF INTEREST

Kerry Ridgeway (Powys/Shropshire)
Last used by drovers some 150 years ago, this ancient
path forges a route through heather moors, woodlands
and bilberry-rich heaths. It is 15 miles (24km) in length
and holds a long tradition as a trade and drove route
from Wales to the lowland English markets.
The route follows a ridgetop overlooking Wales on the
one side and England on the other. It never dips below
1000ft (300m) above sea level, resulting in remarkable
views of up to 70 miles in several directions.

Ironbridge (near Telford, Shropshire)

The world famous, 30-metre-high cast iron bridge was built in 1779 and is set in a stunning location above the Severn gorge.

It is the centrepiece of an area promoted as the 'Birthplace of the Industrial Revolution'. This description is based on the idea that Abraham Darby perfected the technique of smelting iron with coke, in nearby Coalbrookdale, allowing much cheaper production of iron.

The bridge itself, being the first of its kind fabricated from cast iron, and one of the few which have survived to the present day – remains an important symbol, representing the dawn of the industrial age.

The NSD route crosses the gorge two miles further downstream on Coalport Bridge. This is built in a similar style to its more famous cousin and its present form dates from 1818.

Ferry Bridge (Burton upon Trent, Staffordshire)

An ornate, iron suspension bridge built in 1889 (the same year as the Eiffel Tower) to replace the ferry boat which operated here. Ferry Bridge (also called the Stapenhill Ferry Bridge or the Stapenhill Suspension Bridge) is a Victorian pedestrian bridge over the River Trent. The bridge and its extension, the Stapenhill Viaduct, link Burton upon Trent town centre to the suburb of Stapenhill half a mile away on the other side of the river.

The bridge is the first and only one of its kind in Europe to be built to this design.

Beacon Hill (Leicestershire)
With a height of 814ft (248m), it is the second highest point in Leicestershire after Bardon Hill.
The hill is an extinct volcano comprising of some of the oldest rocks (700 million years) found anywhere across the world.
Great views and some very interesting rock formations can be found at the craggy summit, with a toposcope indicating landmarks which can be seen from the summit. These include Lincoln Cathedral and the hills of the Peak District.
The summit is close to the route and is certainly not to be missed.

Wing Maze (Rutland)

Just 100m off the route, this turf cut maze situated on the edge of the village is reputed to be medieval in origin and is one of just eight surviving in England today. Although called a maze, it's actually a labyrinth, unicursal in structure and 14 metres in diameter, with just one grass path that winds back and forth within a circle before finally leading to the centre.

The origin of a turf maze is unclear and there are many myths and legends surrounding the reasoning behind their existence, including references to the classical Cretan labyrinth from the legend of Theseus and the Minotaur. Theseus, son of King Aegeus of Athens used a ball of wool given to him by Ariadne to mark his way through the labyrinth of the Minotaur in Crete, slayed the monster and retraced his steps with the aid of the thread and so to safety.

The Wing maze also follows the 'Chartres' pattern which, as its name suggests, copies the design of pavement mazes found in European Cathedrals.

Burrough Hill (Leicestershire)
An early Iron Age hill fort around 200m above sea level, commands panoramic views over the surrounding countryside for miles around. There has been human activity in the area since at least the Mesolithic period (mid Stone Age) 5,000 – 15,000 years ago.

Thetford Priory (Norfolk)
Extensive remains of an early 12th century monastery.
Thetford Priory is a Cluniac monastic house situated
in the town of Thetford and founded in 1103 by Roger
Bigod of Norfolk. It was one of the most important
monasteries of East Anglia.

Thetford Castle (Norfolk)

Thetford Castle is an impressive remain of a medieval motte and bailey castle in the market town of Thetford. The first castle in Thetford, a probable 11th-century Norman ringwork called Red Castle, was replaced in the 12th century by this much larger motte and bailey castle on the other side of the town. This new castle was largely destroyed in 1173 by Henry II, although the huge motte, the second largest man-made mound in England, remains intact.

Adnams Brewery Tour (Southwold, Suffolk)
Brewery and distillery tours and tastings are available all year round and showcase the town's rich brewing heritage.
Adnams is an independent regional brewery founded in 1872 by George and Ernest Adnams, though the earliest recorded brewing on the Adnams site was in 1396. It produces cask ale, bottled beer, and in 2010, production of gin, vodka and whisky began at their Copper House distillery. Annual production is around 85,000 barrels.

Southwold Pier (Suffolk)
First built in 1900 on the edge of the quintessential Suffolk town, it extends 620ft (190m) into the North Sea.
Whilst many English seaside piers are in decline, the restored Southwold Pier is enjoying renewed popularity.

NORTH-SOUTH DIVIDE DIRECTORY

Campsites:

Gwersylla Tymawr Camping (near Nant yr Arian)
Tymawr, Ponterwyd, SY23 3JR
www.tymawrcamping.co.uk
07980 266523

Dol-Llys Farm Caravan & Camping
B4569, Llanidloes, SY18 6JA
www.dolllyscaravancampsite.co.uk
01686 412694

Woodbatch Camping & Glamping
Middle Woodbatch Farm, Woodbatch Road, Bishops Castle,
SY9 5JS
www.shropshirecampsite.co.uk
01588 630141

Shropshire Camping & Pods
Marshbrook, Church Stretton, SY6 6QE
www.camping-shropshire.co.uk
01694 781515

Small Batch Camp Site
Small Batch, Little Stretton, SY6 6PW
www.smallbatch-camping.co.uk
01694 723358

Lower Hill Campsite (Wenlock Edge)
Lower Hill Farm, Hughley, SY5 6NX
www.lowerhillcampsite.co.uk
07966 491319

Sytche Caravan and Camping Park
Sytche Ln, Much Wenlock, TF13 6NA
www.sytchecaravanandcamping.co.uk
07989 783574

Springslade Lodge
Camp Rd, Cannock, WS12 4PT
www.springsladelodge.co.uk
01785 715091

Whatoff Lodge Farm
Woodhouse Road, Quorn, LE12 8AL
01509 412127

Wingslake Caravan & Camping Park (Rutland)
Wing Hall, Hall Drive, Wing, LE15 8RQ
www.wingslake-caravan-camping-park.business.site
01572 737283

Yarwell Mill Country Park
Mill Rd, Peterborough, PE8 6PZ
www.leisureparksuk.co.uk/yarwell-mill-cambridgeshire
01780 782344

Northey Lodge Touring Park
North Bank, Peterborough, PE6 7YZ
www.northeylodge.co.uk
01733 223918

Fenland Camping and Caravan Park
50 March Rd, Wimblington, March, PE15 0RW
www.fenlandcamping.co.uk
01354 740354

The Dower House Touring Park (Thetford)
East Harling, Norfolk, NR16 2SE
www.dowerhouse.co.uk
01953 717314

Paradise Barn Camping
Wissett Rd, Chediston, Halesworth, IP19 0AY
www.paradise-barn.co.uk
07778 638463

Southwold Caravan Site
Ferry Rd, Southwold, IP18 6ND
www.southwoldcamping.com
01502 722486

Hostels/Bunkhouses:

All Stretton Bunkhouse (Shropshire)
Russells Meadow Ct, All Stretton, SY6 6JW
www.allstrettonbunkhouse.co.uk
01694 722593

Ironbridge Coalport YHA (Shropshire)
John Rose Building, High St, Coalport, Telford, TF8 7HT
www.yha.org.uk/hostel/yha-ironbridge-coalport
0345 371 9325

Refreshments:

Aberystwyth
Numerous options

Poppy's Coffee Shop & Restaurant
Newman's Garden Centre, Capel Dewi, SY23 3HS
www.newmansgarden-centre.co.uk
01970 822313

Nant yr Arian Forest Visitor Centre
Bwlch Nant yr Arian, Ponterwyd, SY23 3AB
www.naturalresources.wales
01970 890453

Llanidloes
Numerous options

Yarborough House
5 Market Square, Bishops Castle, SY9 5BN
www.yarboroughhouse.com
01588 638318

Kirstys
New St, Bishops Castle, SY9 5DQ
01588 638115

Church Stretton
Numerous options

Much Wenlock
Numerous options

Ironbridge
Numerous options

The Tile Press Café
Unit B25 Maws Craft Centre, Jackfield, TF8 7LS
www.mawscraftcentre.co.uk
01952 883190

Penkridge
Numerous options

Springslade Lodge
Camp Rd, Cannock, WS12 4PT
www.springsladelodge.co.uk
01785 715091

Grounds Café Birches Valley (Cannock Chase)
Birches Valley Forest Centre, WS15 2UQ
www.groundscafe.uk/birches-valley
01889 574475

Rugeley
Numerous options

Burton upon Trent
Numerous options

Planters at Bretby
Bretby Ln, DE15 0QS
www.plantersgc.com
01283 703355

Melbourne
Numerous options

St. Joseph's Tea Room, Abbey Grange (E of Thringstone)
Oaks Rd, LE67 5UP
01509 506935

Beacon Hill Café
Breakback Rd, Woodhouse Eaves, LE12 8TA
www.leicscountryparks.org.uk
0116 305 1650

The Buttermarket Cafe
38a Market Pl, Mountsorrel, LE12 7BA
01162 106112

Sileby
Numerous options

Beardsleys Tearoom
2 Brook St, Rearsby, LE7 4YA
www.beardsleystearoom.co.uk
01664 424008

Cafe @ Rutland Water Garden Nursery
Rutland Water Gardens Nursery, nr. Manton, LE15 8RN
www.rutlandnursery.co.uk
01572 498720

Grounds Café Fineshade
Top Lodge, Fineshade, NN17 3BB
www.groundscafe.uk/fineshade
01780 444795

Whittlesey
Numerous options

March
Numerous options

Welney Wetland Centre
Hundred Foot Bank, Welney, PE14 9TN
www.wwt.org.uk/welney
01353 860711

Copper Beech Tearoom
Brandon Country Park Visitor Centre, Bury Rd, Brandon
IP27 0SU
www.brandoncountrypark.org.uk
01842 810185

The Cafe & Pantry (Thetford Forest)
High Lodge Visitors Centre, Thetford Road, IP27 0AF
01842 814042

Thetford
Numerous options

Halesworth
Numerous options

Harbour Café
Southwold Harbour, IP18 6TA
www.southwoldboatyard.co.uk/cafe
01502 722593

Harbour Kiosk
Southwold Harbour, IP18 6ND

Southwold
Numerous options

Bike Shops:

* Denotes bike shop on or within 5 minutes of route.

Summit Cycles*
65 North Parade, Aberystwyth, SY23 2JN
01970 626061

Blazing Bikes* (Nr. Long Mynd)
Shropshire Hills Mountain Bike and Outdoor Pursuit Centre,
Marshbrook, SY6 6QE
01694 781515

Plush Hill Cycles
9A Birchfield Way, Overdale, Telford TF3 5BZ
01952 763274

Cannock Chase Cycle Centre*
Rugeley, WS15 2UQ
01889 575170

Cycling 2000*
Unit 1, Anglesey Business Park
Anglesey Road
Burton on Trent, Staffordshire
DE14 3LX
01283 544669

Pedal power
47 Ashby Rd, Loughborough, LE11 3AA
01509 269663

Oakham Cycle Centre
International House, 2 Barleythorpe Rd, Oakham,
LE15 6NR
01572 757058

Specialized Rutland
Normanton Car Park, Nr Edith Weston, LE15 8HD
01780 720888

Grounds Cycle Centre*
Top Lodge, Fineshade Woods, NN17 3BB
07888 441564

The Cycle Shop*
3 Nene Parade, March, PE15 8TD
01354 656150

Halfords Thetford*
Lime Kiln Ln, Thetford IP24 2BU

Madgetts Cycles
8 Shelfanger Rd, Diss, IP22 4EH
01379 650419

Byways Bicycles
Priory Lane, Darsham, IP17 3QD
01728 668764

Becks Bikes
49 Blyburgate, Beccles, NR34 9TQ
01502 714343

Railway Stations:

In ride order found on or close to the route:

Aberystwyth

Caersws

Newtown

Church Stretton

Telford

Shifnal

Cosford

Penkridge

Rugeley Town

Rugeley Trent Valley

Burton on Trent

Sileby

Oakham

Peterborough

Whittlesey

March

Lakenheath

Brandon

Thetford

Diss

Halesworth

Tough going into the notorious Fenland headwind!

Great trails on the Long Mynd

One of several 1000+ feet climbs heading across Wales

Commanding views from the Iron Age hill fort at Burrough Hill

Mile upon mile of natural and purpose-built trails in Thetford Forest

Remote Welsh Marches

Coalport Bridge is used to cross the Severn Gorge downstream of its more-famous cousin at nearby Ironbridge.

Upland forestry in the Cambrian Mountains

Panoramic views from the Kerry Ridgeway.

NORTH-SOUTH DIVIDE EVENT
MAY 2023

At MTB Epics UK we usually organise at least one supported event each year and for 2023, it was to be a six-day event on the NSD. It also gave me a great excuse to ride the route in its entirety, something I hadn't done for ten years or so!

Part of putting on an event is the pre-event route recce. This is important because things change on such a long route. Some issues we've come across in the past have been major road works, new gas pipeline infrastructure, new housing estates, forestry work, HS2 and rights of way closures.

Quite a few sections on this route have been improved or changed over the last ten years, most notably, changing from what was originally a very difficult hike-a-bike up to the Cefn Croes windfarm to an actual rideable detour, adding an excellent woodland descent into the Ironbridge gorge and a new off-road climb to the top of the Long Mynd, replacing the 30% Asterton Bank road climb.

Other sections that we've altered to improve the route from the original are using the Trent & Mersey canal to enter Burton and several droves in the Fens.

MTB Epics UK Recce Machine - 1000W/52V beast!

Lined up at the start

25 riders were scheduled to start on the promenade in Aberystwyth and almost all managed to reach the North Sea coast six days later despite a few injuries and scrapes! Kudos goes out to Mr Gary Evans who shrugged off a nasty hand injury sustained on Day 1 and then ignored the obvious pain to finish the event – he later required surgery!

The following section is dedicated to the riders who rode the NSD, here is their story in their own words...

THE RIDERS

Sam Piercey

United we stand, divided we fall. The North-South Divide, just an excuse to get some great riding in (apart from the Fens) and test your endurance to pleasure and pain.

Once again, the weather had been booked to deliver dry trails, sweaty climbs and especially stingy stinging nettles.

Obligatory swim in the Irish sea done, quick photo call and off to live another day.

Road to field to trail centre. Cafe stops where you can, corner shop where you can't. No support on this one. Failing to fuel would see you broken on the trail ahead.

The wilderness climbs of Wales, in the scorching sunshine, gave respite on the summits with a steady breeze. The sheep playing an exciting game of chicken on the steep descents.

Onwards to Ironbridge and the Midlands we rode, into busier places and a faster pace.

Our accommodation would vary from tent to pod to B&B. You'd think a pod for the night would seem like a dream but a tent to yourself, for some, was much better.

Fast, flowy trails through the trail centres of Cannock and Thetford on cool mornings, would contrast with the bumpy byways and bridleways under the burning sun.

Nothing would compare to the pain of the Fens. Easy flat spinning was the expectation, but in truth, it was to be monotonous hard pedalling into a strong headwind. Distraction from the pain, on the endless flat and often dead straight roads was hard to invoke. A fine cafe amid the wilderness, was a blessed relief.

The last day and still the sun was shining. Last time to feel that saddle sore. A brisk pace turned into a race to the Jungle Cafe. How long until the end? Onwards through the scrublands, emerging on the river that would take us to the sea, a celebration swim and ice cream.

Another epic done; another challenge complete. What next?

Pods? Some preferred a tent!

Shane Miller

The wifey said she fancied a weekend in Southwold, so I said OK, I'll start in Aberystwyth and meet you there.

So began another chapter in the MTB Epics UK event catalogue, along with a bunch of 20+ other riders.

A coast to coast for me usually involves a swim at the start. At Aberystwyth, this was in fact unexpectedly pleasant, unlike Southwold at the finish where the water was wild and freezing cold. Another dip was had after a very hot ride across Wales on the first day. The campsite we stayed at was situated next to the river Severn and was a great spot for another swim opportunity.

Wales is full of MTB routes with fun descents and epic climbs, but when crossing the Midlands, it's more challenging to find interesting off-road routes. But Vince again, through his years of cycling and now extensive knowledge, created a marvellous route taking in places like Bishops Castle, Much Wenlock and Ironbridge.

Camping at Cannock Chase with a great evening meal at the on-site café was also memorable.

The following morning, we set off for Rutland, the longest (and hottest) day at 86 miles. The campsite was located at Wing Hall and we had the place to ourselves. A short ride to the Horse and Jockey at Manton for a superb meal and a few beers rounded off another tough day.

The 5th day was to become the real challenge though. Rutland to Brandon at 82 miles and across the Fens with a headwind. Whichever way we turned the wind was always against us. But we had a secret weapon, Simon! He got on the front of our group and set a fast pace for the rest of us to try and hang on. Others tried to take their turn on the front but somehow Simon would just appear back on point slicing through the air. Eventually we could see the trees of Thetford Forest and some protection. Finally, we reached our destination of Brandon where life excelled itself, a beer in a jacuzzi followed by a great restaurant meal and a proper bed in a luxury air B&B.

The last day was a 'short' one at 60 miles that began with great fun winding through Thetford Forest. Eventually we could sense the end of our journey as we entered a sandy common with gorse bushes leading towards Walberswick and Southwold.

And guess what, I still got there before wifey!

Thanks to Vince for all his hours spent creating these routes and thanks to all the participants, great companions to ride with.

Ade Tuckley

My little story of the North-South Divide.

This was my first multi-day event and being a fairly long one, I didn't know what to expect. I've been riding for 10 years now (I'm 40 years old) and generally ride up to ten hours a week which includes some local MTB XC races during the spring and summer.

Had I done enough training? What level of fitness would the other riders be at compared to me? Could I ride those distances 6 days in a row? How technical would it be?

I think if you can comfortably ride 100km on a MTB then your fitness level will be good enough for similar events. But could I ride roughly that distance 6 days in a row? Well, yes, I did, but I would say the struggles I had weren't can my legs keep going, it was more can I sit on that saddle tomorrow! The pain is worth it. The fitness level of the other riders turned out to be similar to myself, but it also turned out it didn't really matter.

The technicality of the route I was ok with. I've ridden many trail centres throughout the UK and my skills aren't great, but there wasn't anything I couldn't ride.

I chose to ride my short travel full suspension XC MTB and I think for myself it was a good choice. I think the XC MTB was a good happy medium between a trail MTB and a gravel bike.

I joined up with a couple of guys on day 1 and rode with them all week. It was nice to randomly bump into other riders during the day at cafes and viewpoints and see how everyone was getting on.

The whole experience was amazing. I've done some fairly big one-day rides before but always finished where

I'd started. This was a journey, every day we were going somewhere different and at the end of each day I'd look at the map and think wow!

This ride has really inspired me to do more multi-day rides and I will definitely be checking out what MTB Epics has going on next year. I think if you're not quite ready for bikepacking, this type of event is a great way to start out. The MTB Epics crew looked after us well all week. All the places they arranged for us to stay had decent facilities. If I did the route again there's nothing I'd change, especially the weather which luckily was fantastic all week!

NSD Event Llanidloes

Mark Poole

I have to say from the moment I saw the link to this ride, I was wide eyed and in!

It didn't disappoint; watching the landscape transform, rise, fall and soften into Suffolk. The images of tracks and trails, hills and valleys, are fixed in my memory. A truly great route to experience the beauty of our countryside.

Adam, Chris and Gary

Looking good in finisher's Tshirts

Beach celebration

Celebrate with a dip

Kat and Rocky

Mission complete

We made it!

NORTH-SOUTH DIVIDE

IMAGE CREDITS

All images by MTB Epics UK except:
P.30, Kerry Ridgeway by shropshiresgreatoutdoors. co.uk. Ferry Bridge, Burton upon Trent by Ralph Rawlinson (CC BY-SA 2.0). Old Man Beacon by Kev747 at English Wikipedia (CC BY-SA 3.0). Wing Maze by Wing Community, wingrutland.co.uk. Wing Maze Design by stone-circles. org.uk. Thetford Priory by Tanya Dedyukhina (CC BY-SA 3.0). Thetford Castle by Geni (CC BY-SA 4.0). Adnams Brewery, Southwold by John Winfield (CC BY-SA 2.0). Southwold Pier by KevinScottNL (CC BY-SA 3.0). Coalport Bridge by Peter Lewis at English Wikipedia (CC BY-SA 3.0). All maps are Google Map Data ©2023 United Kingdom

ROUTE FEEDBACK

If you have any local information, for example, trail re-classification, trail closures, bike shops opening or closing, or you know of a worthy section of trail that could fit and improve this route then please let us know and it could be included in future editions of the NSD.
Please contact us at **info@mtbepicsuk.co.uk**

ACKNOWLEDGEMENTS

Firstly, I would like to thank my wife Kathryn, who supports me in having time away to create these guidebooks.

Thanks also to the Northants Outcasts MTB Collective, who've accompanied me on many route recces and to all the random riders I've met on the trails willing to share their local knowledge.

And last but not least, a massive thank you to my good friends Paul and Matt who once again were willing volunteers to help create this route.

ABOUT THE AUTHOR

Vince Major lives in Northamptonshire and has been riding mountain bikes since 1989. His broad MTB experiences range from XC, freeride and downhill at home and abroad. His vast knowledge of good MTB areas in the UK stems from the fact that living in Northants, not being a MTB hotspot itself, has meant travelling to other areas to find and ride the best trails. One advantage of being in a central location means relatively quick and easy access to other parts of the UK.

Vince has also acquired a wealth of experience in organising MTB events and bike trips at home and abroad for friends and club mates. These range from single days out to ten day epics, always with the emphasis on 'having an adventure'.

Other books in the
by Mountain Bike series

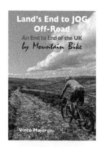

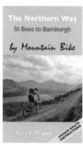

Please contact Vince Major at:
info@mtbepicsuk.co.uk

Milton Keynes UK
Ingram Content Group UK Ltd.
UKHW050721070224
437285UK00007B/75